Tees-side

TROLLEYBUSES

Stephen Lockwood

Series editor Robert J Harley

MP *Middleton Press*

Cover Photograph: The Tees-side trolleybus system relied entirely on single-deck vehicles until the Second World War. In 1944 double-deck utility Sunbeam W trolleybuses were introduced, including Roe-bodied car 11, the third of four vehicles to carry this fleet number over the life of the system. It is seen in Normanby Road in 1959 at one of the more rural parts of the system, although the steelworks at Grangetown are evident in the distance. (J.Copland/Photobus)

Published April 2005

ISBN 1 904474 58 6

© Middleton Press, 2005

Design David Pede

Published by
> *Middleton Press*
> *Easebourne Lane*
> *Midhurst, West Sussex*
> *GU29 9AZ*
Tel: 01730 813169
Fax: 01730 812601
Email: info@middletonpress.co.uk
www.middletonpress.co.uk

Printed & bound by Biddles Ltd, Kings Lynn

CONTENTS

INTRODUCTION & ACKNOWLEDGEMENTS

This trolleybus system, tucked away in the north-east corner of Yorkshire at Tees-side, had only about six miles of route for most of its life and never ran more than about twenty vehicles. Despite this small size it was one of Britain's longest lived and most interesting operators of electric traction. It ran for over fifty years, a feat that only Rotherham and Bradford equalled, and it had survived all other British systems except Bradford when it closed in April 1971.

The origins of the system lay in the iron and steel industry on the south bank of the Tees. It was promoted by local business interests, including the ironmasters, from whose works the trolleybuses drew their power until 1955. There had been no previous tramway development in the area, and the route linked the close-knit communities beside the steelworks. It did not serve a large town centre, the North Ormesby terminus being almost a mile from Middlesbrough's Town Hall.

The Tees-side undertaking had three owners during its lifetime, and for most of its existence was administered by a municipal joint body, the Tees-side Railless Traction Board (TRTB). Apart from vehicle matters, the operation was very stable, with no route developments for the first 30 or so years until the 1950s. The last full decade of its existence was its most energetic in terms of change, including the opening of two route extensions (including Britain's last) at a time when most trolleybus systems were closing. The final change of ownership (or more properly amalgamation) spelt the end for this hitherto pro-trolleybus operation, and the

system closed three years after the new owners took control.

My own first contact with the green Tees-side trolleybuses occurred on a misty Sunday evening in September 1966, following a visit to the once huge Newcastle trolleybus system which would close the following month. The trip I took to Normanby included riding over the temporary diversion brought about by major bridge repairs, which had required new wiring to be specially erected on a half-mile stretch of road. It is a measure of this system's faith in the trolleybus that this was done – any other trolleybus town faced with such a diversion during the mid-1960s would have used this as an excuse to substitute motorbuses permanently on the route. Ironically, a row of traction poles on the northern section of this diversion in Old Middlesbrough Road remains today as a physical reminder of the Tees-side trolleybus system.

Today, the area has been transformed by new road development, mainly the eastward extension of the A66 trunk road. The first third of a mile of the former trolleybus route eastwards from North Ormesby has been obliterated, the Smeaton Street terminus now lying under a road interchange complex associated with the A66 trunk road built in the 1970s. Further east in South Bank, the A66 has scythed through the former route to Grangetown just past Bennett's Corner, the truncated road beyond being now an industrial estate road. In Grangetown, Whitworth Road, once a shopping street which led to the Market Square terminus, now leads off the A66 to the industrial estates, all trace of the Market Square having gone. The rest of the former system, however, through the Grangetown housing estate to Eston and from South Bank to Normanby, is largely as it was when the trolleybuses last ran.

The system's operator is generally referred to by its initials: TRTB – Tees-side Railless Traction Board or TMT – Teesside Municipal Transport. The title of the Board used the hyphenated form of spelling 'Tees-side'. This has been used throughout this book, apart from references to 'Teesside County Borough' and 'Teesside Municipal Transport,' which did not use the hyphen. For readers unfamiliar with the geography of the area, the distinction between the references 'South Bank' and 'south bank' should be pointed out. The former is the name of a township between North Ormesby and Grangetown, whilst the latter is used merely as a generic descriptive term for the area as a whole.

There has been a difficulty in defining the shade of the pale blue/green mix that TMT used as its livery and applied to the trolleybuses from 1968. The livery is described in this book as 'turquoise', with apologies to anyone who may disagree with this interpretation. The TRTB trolleybuses were always referred to by staff as 'cars' and this practice has been perpetuated here.

The photographs take the reader on a tour of the system, commencing at North Ormesby, and concluding with a survey of the rolling stock and other items of interest. I have managed to include at least one view of each of the double-deck vehicles in both original and re-bodied forms, although the relative rarity of views prevents similar coverage of the pre-war single-deck vehicles.

I am grateful to all those photographers who have allowed their work to be reproduced here and to those who responded to requests for information and loan of material. Thanks are due to: Eric Old, for the loan of some very elderly negatives of the single-deck trolleybuses and to Paul Watson, who has again produced some excellent prints from these negatives.

Thanks also go to: David Beach, a long-time friend from my schooldays, who has loaned some of his TRTB material; John Henderson for his recollections of the system in the 1950s and 1960s; the staff of Teesside Archives, who have allowed me access to their TRTB records; and The Industrial Railway Society for permission to quote from their journal.

The maps have been kindly drawn by Roger Smith, who has made an excellent job of interpreting my rough sketch. Roger has adapted the legislation map from those that appeared in John Watson's articles on Tees-side tramway legislation published in Tramway Review and it is shown here with permission from the author and publisher.

Sincere gratitude goes to: John Watson of Hartlepool, for allowing me access to his extensive research into the Tees-side system, including extracts from the minute books of the Board, and for patiently guiding me through the intricacies of the system's pre-history; Philip Battersby of Middlesbrough, auther of books on passenger transport in the area, for the loan of archive photographs and material, and for undertaking specific areas of research; Peter Price of Bradford, one-time TMT trolleybus driver and foreman overhead linesman for the loan of photographs and answering many questions of an operational nature; and Stanley King, also from Bradford, who has again allowed me to select from his collection of excellent photographs. As well as being a noted tram and trolleybus historical author, Stanley has recently been appointed Chairman of the West Yorkshire Passenger Transport Authority. Peter Cardno, Chairman of the Northern Branch of the Omnibus Society, has, together with John, Philip, Peter and Stanley, kindly read over my text and suggested improvements where appropriate. Finally, I must once again acknowledge the crucial part played by my wife Eileen, through her constant support and encouragement, and not least her proof-reading skills.

GEOGRAPHICAL SETTING

The River Tees flows into the North Sea some 40 miles/64km south of the River Tyne at Newcastle. Seven miles upstream, on the south bank, is situated the industrial town of Middlesbrough, and slightly to the west, on the north bank, is the market town of Stockton-on-Tees. Prior to the formation of Teesside County Borough in 1968, (which was itself absorbed into the new County of Cleveland in 1974), the Tees formed the boundary between the North Riding of Yorkshire and County Durham. Thus, Tees-side's trolleybuses ran in the North Riding and they bore that County's registration marks. The area of flatland on the south bank of the river, stretching nine miles eastwards from Middlesbrough to Redcar, is steel-making country and the large furnaces dominate the landscape. The trolleybus route started in North Ormesby, on the south–east edge of Middlesbrough, and ran through the communities of South Bank and Grangetown, where the Bolckow, Vaughan steelworks (which became Dorman Long in 1929) was the main employer. To the south, and forming a contrasting backdrop over the heavily industrialised area, lay the Eston Hills, whence came the ironstone to feed the furnaces.

HISTORICAL BACKGROUND

The establishment of trolleybuses on Tees-side was a rather protracted affair. Electric trams, operated by the Imperial Tramways Company, had reached North Ormesby from Middlesbrough in 1898. Powers to provide a tramway to South Bank and Grangetown were eventually obtained by Imperial Tramways in 1904, following an unsuccessful attempt by a syndicate of local businessmen to construct its own tramway. The 1904 Act included the provision of a bridge to allow the tramway to connect with the existing line at North Ormesby without using the North Eastern Railway level crossing at this point. Despite firm promises and gaining time extensions to these powers, the tramways company never commenced construction of the south bank tramway.

Frustrated by the failure of Imperial Tramways to take up its powers, and anxious to provide transport for the employees of its members, the syndicate, backed by Bolckow, Vaughan and Company Ltd, submitted new proposals. No doubt encouraged by similar trackless developments in Bradford and Leeds, the syndicate applied for, and in 1912 was granted, parliamentary powers for a railless traction route between North Ormesby, South Bank, Eston (via Normanby) and Grangetown. To protect the local passenger services of the North Eastern Railway, the undertaking was not to be permitted any future extension into Middlesbrough, whose boundary at the time was close to the North Ormesby level-crossing. Accordingly the route commenced at the western end of Smeaton Street. The outbreak of war slowed progress but by early 1916 Clough, Smith and Company had erected the poles and wires, apart from the short section from Normanby to Eston which was not proceeded with. Other work included erection of the depot at South Bank near Cargo Fleet and the provision of an adjacent railway bridge to take the route over the North Eastern Railway's Eston branch line. This was included in the scheme so that an existing unsatisfactory level-crossing could be avoided. The road between North Ormesby and South Bank still had toll-bars in operation and these needed to be eliminated. To provide the service, ten single-deck trolley vehicles were ordered from the RET Construction Company Limited. The undertaking was titled 'The North Ormesby, South Bank, Normanby and Grangetown Railless Traction Company'.

However, events were combining to prevent the company from making progress. Wartime conditions and the financial failure of RET caused great delays in the building of the vehicles. By 1919, Middlesbrough successfully sought powers to take into public control the town's tramway system, and with agreement of

TEES-SIDE RAILLESS TRACTION BOARD

Trolleybus wiring as at 31st March 1968

SOUTH BANK

River Tees

Sou
Ba

CARGO FLEET

Cargo Fleet
Iron Works

Goods Siding

BROUGH

'SBRO'RD

Depot

LC

Form

OLD MIDDLE

MIDDLES-

Cargo
Fleet
Lane

SOUTH BANK ROAD
(A 175)

SOUTH BANK ROAD

Cargo Fleet

GEORGE ST

Penny-man St.

High St.

SMEATON ST.

HAMPDEN ST

West Terrace

BR(NE) to Whitby

A

North LC
Ormesby
Road

LANGBAURGH
PLACE

North
Ormesby

Road

Trunk

Longlands

Scale:

0	1/4	1/2	3/4	1 mi
0		0,5		1 km

SCALE EXAGGERATED AT
JUNCTIONS & TURNING CIRC

A After 3/70	B Before 5/38 & after 3/70	C Before 1922	D Before 6/64	E Before 31/3/68	F Before 31/3

A: SMEATON ST. / HAMPDEN ST. / West Terr.

B: M'BRO' RD. / M'BROUGH RD. E. / NORMANBY ROAD

C: WHITWORTH RD. / HOLDEN ST. / Pochin Rd. / BOLCKOW ROAD

D: BIRCHINGTON AVENUE / Kings-ley Rd.

E: BIRCHINGTON AVE. / Fabian Rd.

F: NORMANBY RD. / High / Stre

1922 – 1950

WHITWORTH RD. / Holden St. / BOLCKOW ROAD

Opening dates:-

A - C } 8/11/19
B - F }
C - D   6/4/50
D - E   23/6/64
E - F   31/3/68

Legend

- ⊏⊐ trolleybus wiring
- ====== trolleybus wiring, temporary
- ------ other roads
- ⊢□⊣ railway and station
- LC   level crossing
- —·—·— municipal boundary

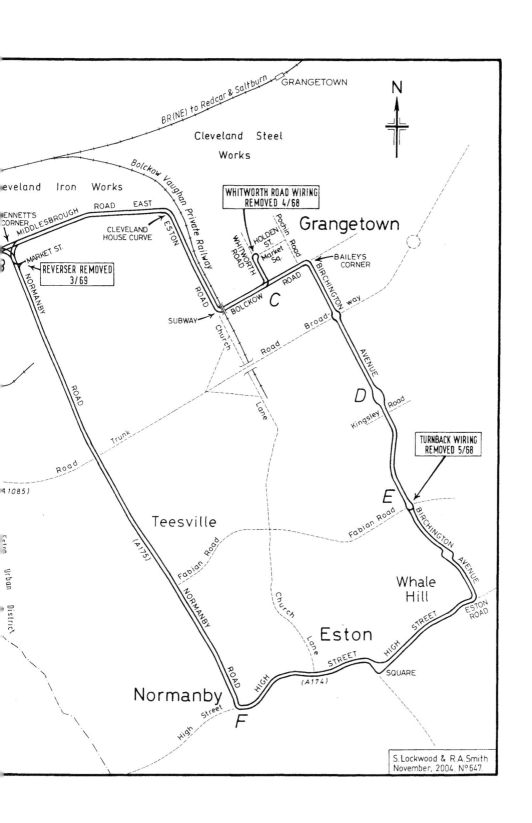

the company, the trolley vehicle system on the south bank. North Ormesby had become part of Middlesbrough County Borough in 1913 (with no effect on the trolley vehicle undertaking's powers), but most of the remainder of the trolley vehicle route lay in Eston Urban District Council's area. To reflect this, the undertaking passed to the management of a joint board, being owned by both Middlesbrough (one third share) and Eston (two thirds share). The new joint undertaking was named the 'Tees-side Railless Traction Board (TRTB). The electric power for the vehicles was to be supplied by Bolckow, Vaughan from its own power station, a situation that survived the Dorman, Long takeover in 1929. In 1947, the section west of the depot began to be supplied by power from the newly formed North Eastern Electricity Board, and the remainder of the system followed in 1955, when Dorman, Long's involvement ceased.

A new company, Railless Ltd, successor to the bankrupt RET Construction Company Ltd, enabled construction of the vehicles to be completed by 1919. The service was finally inaugurated on Saturday 8th November, following a trial run with one of the cars on 19th September and the Board of Trade inspection of the system on 31st October. This was some three years after the wiring and depot had been completed. At the opening ceremony, the Chairman of the Board, Councillor WG Grace, drove the first car out of the depot, followed by the civic party riding to Normanby and Grangetown. Afterwards, the public service commenced which carried almost 6,000 passengers during the day.

"It is a pleasant thought that a little joy might be brought into the lives of the children and old people by opening up to them the fresh air of the Eston Hills. We [the Board] look forward to the time when the system would stretch forth its arms and embrace a much wider area than it does at present." Extract from the speech made by the Chairman of the Board at the opening ceremony of the railless system.

Whilst most of the route ran alongside the steelworks between North Ormesby and Grangetown, the Normanby section, which branched off at Bennett's Corner in South Bank, was nearly two miles long and largely rural, hardly warranting a service at that time. The terrain was generally flat, the only gradients of any note being the approaches to the railway bridge at South Bank, and the dip under another railway bridge near Grangetown, known locally as the subway. The sharp bend adjacent to this bridge added to the difficulty in negotiating this feature. All three termini had tight turning circles in the carriageway, and as time went on, ever increasing traffic caused a worsening problem for the operator at these points.

In 1921, the Imperial Tramways Company undertaking was purchased jointly by Middlesbrough, Stockton and Thornaby Corporations. The resultant Middlesbrough Corporation Transport undertaking always operated quite independently of Middlesbrough's share of the TRTB.

Plans to achieve the original goal of serving Eston came to the fore in 1922 when the Board applied for powers to run a trackless service branching off the existing route near the Grangetown subway, and running along Church Lane to Eston Square. This trackless extension was never proceeded with, the route eventually being inaugurated by the Board using motorbuses. These vehicles had been introduced into the fleet from 1926 to expand services away from the existing trackless service and fend off competition from private motorbus operators. Another, more radical, solution to the Eston question came in 1924, when a dual-mode petrol-electric trolley vehicle capable of running away from the overhead, entered service. This ran between North Ormesby and Eston, operating the short distance from Normanby to Eston Square with the trolley poles lowered and using the petrol engine to generate power to the motor. The vehicle was built to the design of the Board's General Manager, JB Parker, who had previously designed an improved trackless car, of which five were built, to augment the original Railless fleet. Access to the other traffic goal – Middlesbrough town centre - remained unresolved until after 1928, when the railway's legal protection was removed. The following year, the Board's motorbuses commenced running a service into central Middlesbrough, although the desire to extend the overhead wires there remained strong throughout the Board's existence. As proof of this expectation, the destination blinds of all the TRTB trolleybuses had 'Middlesbrough' included on them.

The 1930 Road Traffic Act resulted in the responsibility for bus route licensing (but not trolleybus) passing to independent Area Traffic Commissioners in 1931. The new Northern Commissioner would only allow protection from bus competition for the Board's trolleybus service (by means of a protective fare) if the condition of the fleet was improved within a year. Therefore, to replace the original Railless cars, in 1932 the Board placed in service eight Ransomes, Simms, and Jeffries trolleybuses to a modern design. These carried a striking new livery of light blue and white, a scheme that did not wear well over the years in the harsh atmospheric conditions of the area. It was subsequently replaced by a more durable hedge-green livery.

At this time, Middlesbrough Corporation was proposing to introduce trolleybuses on a large scale, partly to replace its final tram route. The scheme was to include running powers over the TRTB route in North Ormesby. However, although the necessary Act was obtained in July 1933, the trolleybus powers were never exercised. It is quite possible that the future of TRTB would have been rather different if Middlesbrough had gone ahead with some of its routes.

The Tees-side trolleybus operation had long periods where little changed and the 1930s was largely one of these. The outbreak of war, however, led to a great increase in the demand for steel, and therefore the transport of steelworkers. The use of single–deck trolleybuses, a requirement laid down by the Board of Trade in 1919 due to the restrictive clearance at the subway at Grangetown, had obvious limitations on the numbers of passengers that could be carried. The Board, therefore, persuaded the Ministry of Transport to allow double-deck operation by modifying the overhead wiring to hang over the pavement under the subway bridge, thus allowing a trolleybus to pass through at minimal speed with its trolleys pushed down slightly below its roofline. Eight 56-seat utility double-deck trolleybuses duly joined the fleet in 1944, replacing six older vehicles. A further seven double-deckers arrived in 1950, replacing the remainder of the single-deck fleet.

The first major change to the original trolleybus route occurred on 6th April 1950, when a three-quarter of a mile route extension, first proposed in the mid-1930s, was introduced in Grangetown to serve housing developments. This continued along Bolckow Road from its junction with Whitworth Road, via Birchington Avenue to terminate near Kingsley Road. The remainder of the 1950s was another largely stable period for TRTB, in marked contrast to the next decade that proved positively action-packed. The poor body condition of the 15-strong fleet resulted in major investment, and between 1960 and 1965 the whole fleet was re-bodied. Another route extension opened on 23rd June 1964, when the Grangetown service was taken a distance of one-third of a mile further along Birchington Avenue to turn at the junction with Fabian Road, again as a result of new housing development. The longer-term aim of the Board was to link up the Grangetown and Normanby services, by finally creating a circular service via Eston, and eliminating the increasingly unsafe turn at the Normanby terminus. Powers for this route were sought and eventually granted, despite intense opposition from United Automobile Services who had a major stake in the motorbus service in Eston. Interestingly, any application by the Board to use motorbuses for this route would never have succeeded, because of United's existing three motorbus route licences in Eston. TRTB, therefore, had a major incentive to keep its trolleybuses in operation. More new overhead wiring, temporary in this case, was necessary when the Board's bridge over the railway at South Bank needed re-building. A half-mile diversion over the level-crossing was wired up and used between March and October 1966. On re-opening, the re-built bridge was transferred from the ownership of the Board to the North Riding County Council.

Whilst work on the Eston extension,

Britain's last major new trolleybus route, was progressing, the future of the undertaking was decided by the forthcoming formation of Teesside County Borough, an amalgamation of local authorities in the area. Thus the three municipal bus operations on Tees-side were merged to take effect from Ist April 1968. From that date, TRTB would join Middlesbrough and Stockton Corporations to form Teesside Municipal Transport (TMT) an organisation of which the trolleybus interests would inevitably form a very small part. In view of the widespread closure of trolleybus installations throughout the country at this time, it was hard to see how this 15 vehicle - eight mile system could survive.

The Board pressed on with its new route and it was opened for traffic on Sunday, 31st March 1968 – the very last day of the Board's existence. The operation which passed to TMT was a basic two route service from North Ormesby, diverging in South Bank to run to Eston via Grangetown and back via Normanby or vice-versa. Evidence of the new ownership came when the fleet was painted in the new TMT livery. This was an unusual turquoise shade, which did not suit the vehicles at all.

Whilst the new owners failed to commemorate the 50th anniversary of trolleybus operation in 1969, they did set about improvements and renewals of the overhead wiring and the fleet. TMT publicly aimed to continue trolleybus operation until 1973, when major road improvements would necessitate the abandonment of operation. Five trolleybuses from Reading Corporation joined the fleet in March 1969 to replace a similar number of wartime vehicles. This purchase was surrounded in controversy, and their subsequent service history in Tees-side was far from happy as mentioned elsewhere in this book.

Tees-side's trolleybuses began the 1970s by having to give up the existing North Ormesby terminus and retreat 200 yards along Smeaton Street. Here, they turned by way of a new, well designed triangular reverser into Hampden Street. This alteration, coming into use on 2nd March 1970, was caused by the encroaching major road improvements, and brought to an end almost 51 years of regular use of the original terminus.

Several problems now emerged. The reliability of the vehicles was seen as a cause for great concern, especially in the winter months and this, combined with shortages of staff, resulted in increasing motorbus operation of trolleybus services. Trolleybuses were rarely seen in operation after 7pm. TMT decided to cease trolleybus operation at the earliest opportunity and accordingly the last normal passenger carrying trolleybuses ran on Sunday 4th April 1971. A civic ceremony, when the vehicles made their final appearance on the road, took place a fortnight later on 18th April. So ended one of Britain's smallest and longest-lived trolleybus operations. Only the Bradford system survived it, succumbing in March 1972.

Parliamentary Acts and Orders

The North Ormesby, South Bank, Normanby and Grangetown Railless Traction Act, 1912

The Tees-side Railless Traction Board (Extension of Routes) Order, 1923 (Proposed)

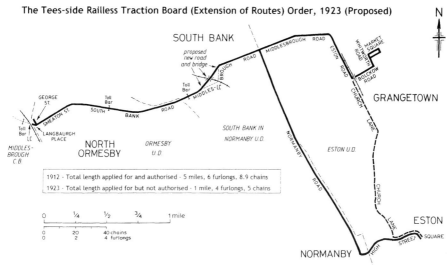

1912 - Total length applied for and authorised - 5 miles, 6 furlongs, 8.9 chains

1923 - Total length applied for but not authorised - 1 mile, 4 furlongs, 5 chains

Subsequent Additions

1. **The Teesside Railless Traction Board (Additional Routes) Order, 1949**

2. **The Teesside Railless Traction Board (Additional Route) Order, 1961**

3. **The Teesside Railless Traction Board (Trolley Vehicles) Order, 1963**

4. **The Teesside Railless Traction Board (Trolley Vehicles) Order, 1966**

Legend (both maps)

- trolleybus route authorised
- trolleybus route proposed but not authorised
- trolleybus route constructed under earlier legislation
- other roads
- railway
- municipal boundary

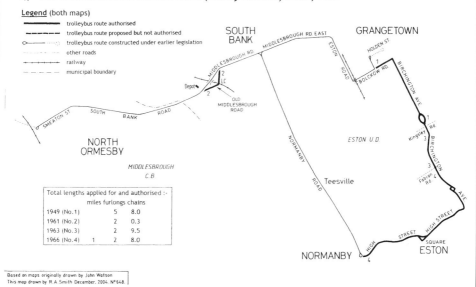

Total lengths applied for and authorised :-

	miles	furlongs	chains
1949 (No.1)		5	8.0
1961 (No.2)		2	0.3
1963 (No.3)		2	9.5
1966 (No.4)	1	2	8.0

Based on maps originally drawn by John Watson

This map drawn by R.A. Smith December, 2004. N° 648.

TRACKLESS CARS

1.	Crowds gather at Cargo Fleet to witness the opening of the system on 8th November 1919. Car 10 is emerging from the depot. (TMT collection)

2.	Car 6 takes an official party round the turning loop at Normanby terminus on opening day. (R.Marshall coll.)

3.   This is an early view showing car 9 beginning the ascent over the Board's railway bridge, showing the bracket arm overhead construction and the enclosed rear platform of these vehicles. (Teesside Archives)

TROLLEYBUS SECTION

FARES LIST

10th JULY, 1966

CHILDREN

(over 3 and under 15 years of age)

———

Any 3d. or 4d. Stage	...	**2d**
Any 5d. or 6d. Stage	...	**3d**
Any 7d. or 8d. Stage	...	**4d**
Any 9d. Stage	... ...	**5d**

SINGLE FARES

Stage No.											
2	NORTH ORMESBY										
3	3	DOVER STREET									
4	4	3	CARGO FLEET OFFICES								
5	5	4	3	SOUTH BANK (Station Road or Bennett's Corner)							
6	6	5	4	3	BRANCH END or CLEVELAND HOUSE						
7	7	6	5	4	3	LYRIC SQUARE or WHITWORTH ROAD					
8	8	7	6	5	4	3	GRANGETOWN (KINGSLEY ROAD)				
9	9	8	7	6	5	4	3	GRANGETOWN (FABIAN ROAD)			
10	6	5	4	3	4	5	6	7	LIBRARY/BATHS		
11	7	6	5	4	5	6	7	8	3	TEESVILLE	
12	8	7	6	5	6	7	8	9	4	3	NORMANBY

4.   The prototype Straker-Clough trackless car 17 poses at the foot of the railway bridge at South Bank opposite the depot. Further details of this car are contained in the caption to photograph 100.(AEI/J.S.King coll.)

5.   Straker car 17 meets Railless car 7 in Normanby Road, South Bank, looking north. (Tramway & Railway World)

6.   The end for the original batch of trackless cars came in 1932 when the survivors were replaced by eight modern Ransomes trolleybuses, to satisfy conditions imposed by the Traffic Commissioner. In May 1932, old car 1 is posed outside the depot with its replacement in this highly symbolic view. (TMT coll.)

NORTH ORMESBY

7.   The western terminus of the system was at North Ormesby, which was known as 'Doggy' to the crews and locals. The turning circle was situated at the west end of Smeaton Street, at its junction with Langbaurgh Place and West Terrace. The turn was very tight and was negotiated by applying full left lock as if turning into West Terrace, then full right lock to make the turn back into Smeaton Street. Rebuilt utility car 18 (the first to be so treated) is seen in 1957 starting the manoeuvre and is following an un-rebuilt example around the circle. Note the signal-light apparatus in the top right-hand corner of the nearside windscreen. (J.S.King)

Route indication signal-lights

TRTB trolleybuses displayed a route indication in the form of a signal-light. On double-deck vehicles this was placed in the top corner of the nearside windscreen. The system seems to have been discontinued in the late-1950s and the lights were never carried on the Roe re-bodied cars. The indications were:- Red – North Ormesby; Green – Normanby; Blue – Grangetown.

8.   Turning one of the longer ex-Reading vehicles at the North Ormesby circle was particularly difficult. This one, at the same point as the previous view, appears to have mounted the pavement with its nearside front wheel. This is a rare view of car 8, which was only in service in Tees-side for three months, between March and June 1969. (Photobus)

9.   Re-bodied car 10 completes the turn (hopefully avoiding the cyclist) on 14th August 1964, with Smeaton Street in the left background. If it were not for the overhead wires and the trolley booms, it might be assumed that the vehicle had come along West Terrace to turn right into Smeaton Street. (J.Copland/A.D.Packer)

Alteration to Stopping Places.

NORMANBY ROUTE.

Passengers are requested to observe that on and after SATURDAY, DECEMBER 5th, the stopping place at Cromwell Road will be withdrawn.

The stopping place at the "Empire" will be moved one pole nearer Cromwell Road, and will serve both these points.

The workmen's stage at Cromwell Road will in future be at the new stop.

A new stopping place has been made at Belmont Avenue midway between the Trunk Road and Teesville.

December, 1936.

10.   The North Ormesby terminal stop was situated outside Rudsdale's shop, where utility car
18 is seen in the early 1950s. (R.Marshall)

11.   North Ormesby period piece. 1950 Sunbeam car 4
stands with rebuilt utility car 18 at the terminus. Rounding
the corner from the Middlesbrough direction is one of the
Board's Leyland Titan motorbuses on the 'T' bus service from
Middlesbrough to Eston via Teesville (on Normanby Road).
A United Bristol K bound for Redcar is waiting at the traffic
lights in North Ormesby Road.   (Roy Brook)

12.   A bleak wintry scene looking along Smeaton Street is
depicted, with car 1 waiting to depart. Note the partially glazed
emergency door which accommodated a platform to allow
maintenance staff access to the trolley booms, and the aperture
in the offside corner panel to store the bamboo trolley retrieval
pole. The date is 30th December 1961. (P.Battersby)

13.   On 26th January 1969, car 6 has unloaded its passengers at North Ormesby and is entering the turning circle. Note that the 'Turning Circle' illuminated sign below the lower-deck rear window has been switched on by the driver. From 1934, the junction was controlled by traffic-lights, and for safety reasons trolleybuses were protected during the turning process, all conflicting traffic being held by red lights. The skate in the overhead which activated this feature can be seen some yards in front of the short bracket arm. There was a second skate further round the turning circle which restored the normal light sequence. (P.Battersby)

14.   A wider view of the Smeaton Street terminus is shown here, with ex-Reading car 12 at the terminal stop on 30th March 1969. Today this entire scene has disappeared, being replaced with approach roads leading to the A66. (J.Copland/A.D.Packer)

15.   The initial stages of the A66 road construction resulted in the North Ormesby terminus being moved 200 yards along Smeaton Street to the junction with Hampden Street. Here, a reversing triangle was erected using modern fittings, including a curved segment on the exit wiring. This came into use on 2nd March 1970. The reverser is shown under construction using the ex-Rotherham tower wagon, whilst car 5 uses the wiring from the existing terminus. (P.Price)

16.   The new terminal arrangement is shown here. Car 16 is at the end of the wires in Smeaton Street before reversing into Hampden Street, whilst car 3, in the distance, is at the new loading stop. A section of outbound wiring towards the old terminus was retained to allow a vehicle to shunt back and enable a following vehicle to proceed in front, as demonstrated here with car 2 on the left. Note that car 16 carries a pseudo-Sunbeam badge on its front panel, and the round speed restriction '10' plates in the overhead layout. (J.S.King)

17.   Having reversed into Hampden Street, car 5 prepares to pull forward to the new terminal stop in Smeaton Street. In the foreground is the ex-Cardiff Corporation tower wagon purchased earlier in 1970. Note that insulators have been placed near the end of the wiring to prevent a vehicle reversing too far. (J.S.King)

18.   Car T295 (17) stands at the new terminal stop with the truncated end of Smeaton Street in the background. Its booms are on the curved segment. The Teesside Municipal Transport fleetname can be seen on the cream band above the lower-deck windows. The original placement of this was below the lower-deck windows, but later repaints had the version shown here which was a clearer display. The ex-Reading cars always had the TMT name in the lower position. (S.Lockwood coll.)

19.   Slightly further east, car 7 proceeds along Smeaton Street towards the terminus in March 1962. (R.F.Mack/C.W.Routh)

20.   The eastern end of Smeaton Street at Pennyman Street is shown here, with car 11 passing tower wagon BAJ 846. This was a 1939 Leyland Tiger converted from bus 25 in 1958. It was the Board's first oil-engined bus and was withdrawn in 1965. (J.Fozard)

CARGO FLEET

21.   Having left North Ormesby, the route proceeded through the heavy industrial area of Cargo Fleet where car 10 is seen between Smeaton Street and Cargo Fleet Lane. In the background, there was an un-gated level crossing carrying an industrial railway across the road. The road sign warning of this is on the left. (J.Fozard)

22.   Heading towards North Ormesby in South Bank Road near Cargo Fleet Lane in the mid-1960s is car 3. Today, the road peters out behind the camera and the remainder of the route into North Ormesby has been obliterated by the A66 trunk road. (J.Fozard)

23.   The section of South Bank Road from Cargo Fleet Lane towards the depot is quite wide and includes grass verges. The road widening was carried out in 1951. Trolleybuses could attain high speeds on this section on the concrete road surface. Car 1 approaches the junction with Cargo Fleet Lane travelling west in March 1962. (R.F.Mack/C.W.Routh)

24.   Cars 5 (left) and 7 negotiate flooding along South Bank Road. Such occurrences required extreme care by the driver to avoid electrical damage to the vehicle. (P.Price)

25.   The main offices of the Dorman Long steelworks were known as Cargo Fleet Offices, and were near to the TRTB depot. Despite the name, they were situated just east of the Middlesbrough/Eston boundary at Spencer Brook and were thus in South Bank, not Cargo Fleet. Steel workers head for home in this view outside the main office building showing cars 3 and 11. (R.Marshall)

DEPOT & BRIDGE

26.   The TRTB depot and head office, situated at Middlesbrough Road South Bank, was a single storey building adjacent to the railway bridge. There were three doorways, and originally each of these was wired. Three different types of vehicle, each with a differing livery style, are posed at the entrance. From left to right, these are an original Railless, an ex-Rhondda Brush car and the prototype Straker. (R.J.Harley coll.)

27.   Forty years on from the previous photograph, newly re-bodied car 7 is posed in the depot doorway in mid-1963. As can be seen, by this time only the centre door was wired. (J.Fozard)

28.   A wider viewpoint looking east in September 1959, with car 16 passing. In the background can be seen the overhead 'siding' on the east side of the building, as seen in photograph 31. (J.Copland/A.D.Packer)

WHITSUNTIDE HOLIDAYS

1938.

RAILLESS SECTION

Ordinary SERVICE will be run throughout the Holidays with EXTRA CARS on Monday and Tuesday, as required.

MOTOR OMNIBUS SECTION
MIDDLESBROUGH—ESTON

Ordinary SERVICE will be run throughout the Holidays with EXTRA BUSES on Monday and Tuesday, as required.

WORKMEN'S TICKETS.

These will NOT be issued on WHIT Monday; other days at usual times.

SPECIAL RETURN FARES FOR CHILDREN.

During School Holidays only, a Special Fare of 3d. RETURN will be made for Children under 14 years of age travelling between Queen's Square or North Ormesby to Grangetown, Normanby or Eston.

RETURN JOURNEY TO BE MADE ON
DAY OF ISSUE.

SOUTH BANK,

MAY 31st, 1938.

JORDISON & CO., LTD., PRINTERS, MIDDLESBROUGH.

29.   Looking in the opposite direction, this view shows the circle of wiring and connections outside the depot which allowed vehicles to enter or leave the depot in either direction. This arrangement dated from 1951, when the road was widened. Car 7 negotiates the layout in 1961. Note the Dorman Long main offices in the background, and the redundant frog for the 'siding' which had recently been dismantled. (J.S.King)

30.   We glimpse inside the depot on Saturday, 30th March 1968. Vehicles reversed in and drove out. There were additional independent sets of wiring within the building. In view is the visiting Brighton trolleybus (see photograph 116), and, on the right, the first two trolleybuses (cars 12 and 13) painted in the new Teesside Municipal Transport turquoise livery. (D.A.Jones/London Trolleybus Preservation Society)

31.   Seen parked under the overhead 'siding' alongside the eastern side of depot in the early 1950s is utility car 11 with car 6. The siding was removed about 1960 when an extension to the depot offices was built. Car 11 has the same style of upper-deck cream relief that was applied to the 1950 Sunbeams. (D.A.Jones/London Trolleybus Preservation Society)

32.   It was common for a spare trolleybus to be parked outside the depot facing South Bank. On a very wet 31st March 1969, the former car 10, displaced by the ex-Reading vehicles and re-numbered 19, is seen in this position whilst being used as a driver training vehicle. It was withdrawn shortly afterwards. In TMT days, the depot was known officially as 'South Depot' (even though it was the most northerly of TMT's three depots) and initially, trolleybuses in TMT livery carried a small white 'S' below the fleet number to signify this. (P.Battersby)

33.   This view of car T285 on the open area adjacent to the depot shows the vehicle undergoing repairs, which includes replacement of the front dash panelling. In the right background can be seen an ex-Reading vehicle that has already been withdrawn from service and stored in the open. (P.Price)

34. Car 4 with a capacity load pauses at the stop opposite the depot. The road in the background is Old Middlesbrough Road which led to the level crossing over the railway. This road was wired in 1966 when the bridge was temporarily closed and presumably some traction pole re-planting would have taken place by then (see photographs 38 to 41). (Photobus)

35. The railway over-bridge at South Bank was built and owned by the Board under the provisions of the 1912 Act to avoid operation over the level crossing. Re-built utility car 10 is seen commencing the climb from the depot in August 1961 with a re-bodied car of the same type following in the distance. Note one of the Board's motorbuses leaving the parking area beside the depot. Unlike the trolleybuses, the motorbuses were parked in the open-air.
(J.Copland/A.D.Packer)

INCREASED
EARLY MORNING SERVICE.

On and after MONDAY, DEC. 18th

early morning trolley buses will run as follows,
MONDAY to SATURDAY inclusive :-

From NORTH ORMESBY—

To SOUTH BANK	-	5-15 a.m. and every 5 minutes
,, GRANGETOWN	-	5-15 a.m. and every 10 minutes
,, NORMANBY	-	5-20 a.m. and every 10 minutes

with usual additional cars until 8-10 a.m. then ordinary service.

From GRANGETOWN—

To NORTH ORMESBY   5-25 a.m. and every 10 minutes until 8-25 a.m., 8-38 a.m. then ordinary service.

From NORMANBY—

To NORTH ORMESBY   5-30 a.m. and every 10 minutes until 8-30 a.m. then ordinary service.

GENERAL MANAGER'S OFFICE,
    SOUTH BANK—11th December, 1939.

JORDISON & CO., LTD., PRINTERS, MIDDLESBROUGH.

36.   Breasting the summit on 17th March 1966, car 11 crosses the railway before descending towards South Bank. (P.Battersby)

37.   An early view of the bridge, with a Railless car crossing from the east. The bracket arm overhead suspension on the bridge was later replaced by span wiring, as seen in the previous photographs. (Tramway and Railway World)

THE 1966 DIVERSION

38.   For eight months, between 19th March and 30th October 1966, the Board took the highly unusual step of diverting the trolleybus service owing to the temporary closure of the bridge for renewal work. New wiring, mainly supported on double bracket arms, was erected over a half-mile diversion. This branched off the normal route opposite the depot along Old Middlesbrough Road, crossed the level crossing, then turned north, re-joining the route at the other end of the bridge. This view shows the new junction arrangements opposite the depot. Note that the running wires on the bridge ramp have been removed. Car 10 approaches the depot from the diversion in July 1966. (J.S.King)

39.   Car 17, bound for North Ormesby, proceeds along Old Middlesbrough Road on the diversion. In the distance, one of the Board's motorbuses is negotiating the railway crossing. (J.S.King)

40.　On the first day of trolleybus operation on the diversion, 21st March 1966, car 4 negotiates the level crossing which the bridge was built to avoid. The railway was once the North Eastern Railway branch line to Eston, whose passenger service ceased in 1929. By 1966 it ran only to South Bank, serving factories and the gas works. Ironically, the branch was formally closed to all traffic in early October 1966 whilst the diversion was still in operation. In December 1925, the Board's Halley tower wagon, hauling a broken-down trackless car, had become stuck on this crossing. The 7.42pm train from Middlesbrough to Eston collided with the tower wagon, the body of which was reduced to matchwood. Fortunately there were no casualties. (P.Battersby)

41.　Old Middlesbrough Road is seen from the north-eastern end on 19th March 1966 with the foot of the bridge ramp on the right. This was just prior to the new wiring being connected to the main route. The traction poles in view along Old Middlesbrough Road still stand today, albeit without their bracket arms. A trolleybus-replacement motorbus enters the scene from the right. This was the last day that any traffic operated over the old bridge, and on the following day (20th), motorbuses operated the trolleybus service via the diversion pending final overhead wiring adjustments. (P.Battersby)

SOUTH BANK BEYOND THE BRIDGE

42.   Beyond the north-eastern end of the bridge, the trolleybus route entered the built-up area of South Bank, known locally as 'Slaggy Island', a rather disparaging reference to its iron and steel origins. Ransomes car 3, bound for North Ormesby, is seen in Middlesbrough Road in the late 1940s. (R.Marshall)

43.   Over a decade later than the previous photograph, and looking in the opposite direction, car 6 has descended from the bridge and turned along Middlesbrough Road towards South Bank centre. (R.F.Mack/C.W.Routh)

44.   A view of Middlesbrough Road, South Bank showing car 11 heading west. Note the bracket arm suspension of the overhead wiring. (J.Fozard)

LAST CARS

Notice is hereby given that commencing Sunday, 19th November, the last through Trolley Buses will run as follows :—

	SUNDAY to FRIDAY.	SATURDAYS.
From NORTH ORMESBY :—		
To Grangetown - -	10-35 p.m.	10-45 p.m.
,, Normanby - -	10-35 p.m.	10-45 p.m.
,, Cargo Fleet & Depot	10-39, 10-44 and 10-55 p.m.	10-55 p.m.
From GRANGETOWN :—		
To North Ormesby -	10-35 p.m.	10-35 p.m.
,, South Bank & Depot -	10-45 and 10-55 p.m.	10-44, 10-52 & 11-5 p.m.
From NORMANBY :—		
To North Ormesby -	10-35 p.m.	10-35 p.m.
,, South Bank & Depot -	10-55 p.m.	10-40, 10-48, 10-56 & 11-5

LAST MOTOR BUSES :

Queen's Square to Eston (Daily)	-	10-30 p.m.
,, ,, ,, South Bank (Daily)	-	11-0 p.m.
Eston to Queen's Square (Daily)	-	10-28 p.m.
,, ,, South Bank (Daily)	-	10-58 p.m.

SOUTH BANK—14th Nov., 1939.

JORDISON & CO., LTD., PRINTERS, MIDDLESBROUGH.

45.   Another look at Middlesbrough Road, this time we are looking west with car 17 near Princess Street approaching Bennett's Corner. (J.Fozard)

46.   At the centre of South Bank was Bennett's Corner, where the Normanby route branched off the Grangetown service. The overhead wiring layout dated from May 1938, when provision was made to allow trolleybuses to operate the peak hour service from Normanby to Grangetown or vice-versa which was introduced at that time. Looking towards Grangetown, utility car 13 is seen in Middlesbrough Road East prior to crossing the junction towards North Ormesby. The main Grangetown loading stop is behind the vehicle on the left. Today, Middlesbrough Road East ends just beyond Bennett's Corner where the new A66 road crosses through. (P.Battersby coll.)

47.   Rush hour at South Bank - this view of Bennett's Corner is looking along Normanby Road on a dismal 11th August 1961. Two re-built utility vehicles are seen, both working on the peak hour Grangetown Square to Normanby service. On the left car 10 is turning from Middlesbrough Road East into Normanby Road, whilst car 15 waits at the traffic lights before turning right towards Grangetown Square. Its conductress is standing by the pull-frog handle ready to facilitate this manoeuvre. This view records how the rear end of a re-built utility looked. (J.S.King)

48.   A view of car 13 which has turned from the North Ormesby direction towards Normanby on Friday 8th June 1963. To make this manoeuvre its trolleys have passed through the only automatic frog on the Tees-side system. This was set for Normanby and drivers of Grangetown bound cars changed the frog setting by applying power to a skate in the overhead. (J.S.King)

49.　Following the formation of Teesside Municipal Transport in 1968, a programme of overhead wiring improvements was instituted which included the removal of wiring not in regular use. Thus, the south to east wiring connections at Bennett's Corner, no longer required following the demise of the peak-hour 'local' service, were taken down in early 1970. The junction therefore reverted to its pre-1938 layout. In early 1971, ex-Reading car T289 (formerly 9) turns from Middlesbrough Road into Normanby Road showing the plain wiring that replaced the junction. By this time, during the last few months of operation, the automatic frog at this point was defective and the conductors of Grangetown-bound vehicles were required to operate the frog by hand. In practice, the North Ormesby-Grangetown-Eston service was operated by motorbuses and trolleybuses were only operated on the North Ormesby-Normanby-Eston route. (P.Battersby)

50.　To allow trolleybuses to turn at South Bank, a reversing triangle was erected in September 1942 alongside the Co-op Store in Normanby Road at Market Street. This earlier scene shows the original method of reversing at this location, using the main wires and the highly flexible Estler trolleybase. Prototype Straker-Clough car 17 demonstrates the manoeuvre. (Tramway and Railway World)

51.   Car 5 is seen having reversed into Market Street during an enthusiasts' tour in April 1968. The reverser was removed in mid-March 1969 as part of the upgrade of the system's overhead wiring facilities. In the event, the actual removal was prompted by a spectacular dewirement at this point which brought down most of the fittings! The 'Circular – N' destination being displayed was used by vehicles working a short-lived peak-hour service introduced with the Eston extension. It ran from Bennett's Corner via Normanby to Eston, returning via Grangetown. A corresponding 'Circular – G' service ran in the opposite direction. (M.J.Henderson)

TOWARDS NORMANBY

52.   From Bennett's Corner, the Normanby route ran for almost two miles along Normanby Road to the terminus. Two cars in TMT livery are shown near the former Empire Cinema, South Bank. Car 4 is in the foreground loading passengers whilst car 1 is proceeding towards Bennett's Corner. (Photobus)

53.   The west side of Normanby Road was largely residential as shown in this early view featuring Straker-Clough car 19 leaving South Bank towards Normanby. (P.Battersby coll.)

54.　Almost 40 years on from the previous photograph, the scene is still semi-rural in this summer 1957 view.　Car 3 approaches the Trunk Road en route to Normanby. (J.S.King)

TIME TABLE

MUNICIPAL TRANSPORT

FROM JUNE, 1946 UNTIL FURTHER NOTICE.

GRANGETOWN ROUTE

NORTH ORMESBY TO GRANGETOWN			GRANGETOWN TO NORTH ORMESBY			
Monday—Thursday	Saturday	Sunday	Monday—Thursday	Friday	Saturday	Sunday

NORMANBY ROUTE

NORTH ORMESBY TO NORMANBY			NORMANBY TO NORTH ORMESBY			
Monday—Thursday	Saturday	Sunday	Monday—Thursday	Friday	Saturday	Sunday

(d—to or from DEPOT)　*(sb—to SOUTH BANK)*

PASSING TIMES from N. ORMESBY		PASSING TIMES from GRANGETOWN		PASSING TIMES from N. ORMESBY		PASSING TIMES from NORMANBY	
CARGO FLEET OFFICES	5 mins. later	CLEVELAND HOUSE	4 mins. later	CARGO FLEET OFFICES	5 mins. later	TEESVILLE	2 mins. later
SOUTH BANK	9 ,, ,,	SOUTH BANK	7 ,, ,,	SOUTH BANK	9 ,, ,,	LIBRARY	5 ,, ,,
CLEVELAND HOUSE	12 ,, ,,	CARGO FLEET OFFICES	10 ,, ,,	LIBRARY	12 ,, ,,	SOUTH BANK	8 ,, ,,
				TEESVILLE	15 ,, ,,	CARGO FLEET OFFICES	12 ,, ,,

55.   Just less than half-way from South Bank to Normanby, the route crossed the A1085 Middlesbrough to Redcar Trunk Road. Car 7 crosses the traffic light-controlled junction on a journey from Normanby. Bracket arm overhead suspension was initially a feature on Normanby Road. (R.Marshall)

56.   A large portion of Normanby Road between South Bank and Fabian Road was gradually widened in 1962/1963. This view shows these works in progress, with newly re-bodied car 12 using the bracket arms which would soon be replaced by span wiring. This will be supported by the newly–planted poles on the right. The old traction poles would disappear when the carriageway on the right opened and the outbound wiring was re-located above the new part of the road. The replacement poles were obtained from London Transport and South Shields. (J.S.King)

NORMANBY ROAD IN THE 1940s

57.   Eric Old was able to capture some very rare images of trolleybuses in Normanby Road during the 1940s. This is Leyland car 9 during World War II, complete with the blackout headlamp masks and white edging paint. Views of this batch of vehicles in service in Tees-side are extremely rare. (A.E.Old)

58.   Ransomes car 1 is seen operating in the severe winter of 1947. The location is near to the Trunk Road junction. Note the Fare Stage sign. (A.E.Old)

59.   A similar view at the same location as the previous view, but looking in the opposite direction, shows the unique car 14 braving the snow and ice in 1947. Note how the trolley booms taper inwards. This was a consequence of being spaced two feet apart on the trolley base whilst being used on 18 inch spaced wiring. (A.E.Old)

NORMANBY TERMINUS

60.   At the Normanby terminus alighting stop, car 10 is seen whilst performing driver-training duties in 1967. Note the typical slim-line sheet metal TRTB trolleybus stop sign. These replaced the earlier design of dark blue enamel signs with white lettering which suffered from premature corrosion. (J.S.King)

61.	The Normanby terminus was a tight turning circle at the main crossroads in the village. Car 11 prepares to make the turn. The waiting shelter at the loading stop can be seen on the left. (J.S.King)

62.	Utility car 15 has got itself into bother whilst negotiating the circle. Its positive trolley boom has dewired and become jammed in the wiring which accounts for the alarming list to the vehicle. The crew of tower wagon VN 1962, are attempting to sort out the problem. This vehicle was a 1930 Leyland Lion with Leyland body which was formerly bus No. 25 in the Board's fleet, being converted into a tower wagon in 1941 and withdrawn in 1958. It was replaced by another bus conversion BAJ 846, as shown in photograph 20. (The Northern Echo/J.Banks coll.)

63.   Car 7 appears in this early view of Normanby terminal loop. Note the tight turning circle and the caravan on the left. (R.J. Harley coll.)

64.   A rare view of the rear-end of the 1942 car 14 at Normanby, shows the design of the rear entrance. (H.V.Jinks/A.E.Old coll.)

MUNICIPAL TRANSPORT

TEES-SIDE RAILLESS TRACTION BOARD.

TROLLEYBUS TIME TABLE

FROM NOV., 1958 UNTIL FURTHER NOTICE.

GRANGETOWN ROUTE | NORMANBY ROUTE

NORTH ORMESBY TO GRANGETOWN			GRANGETOWN TO NORTH ORMESBY			NORTH ORMESBY TO NORMANBY			NORMANBY TO NORTH ORMESBY		
Monday—Friday	Saturday	Sunday	Monday—Friday	Saturday	Sunday	Monday—Friday	Saturday	Sunday	Monday—Friday	Saturday	Sunday
5-30 am	As Mon.—Fri. until 12-10 pm	5-30 am 5 40 5 50 6 08 6 25 6 45 7 05 7 35 7 45 8 25 9 04 9 26 9 50 10 14 10 38 11 02 11 20	5-30 am	As Mon.—Fri. until 12-30 pm	5-40 am 5 50 6 05 6 10d 6 26 6 45 7 03 7 25 7 55d 8 05 8 45 9 20 9 44 10 08 10 32 10 56 11 20	5-35 am	As Mon.—Fri. until 11-55 am	5 15d 5 20d 6-05 am 6 45 6 55d 7 25 8 05 8 38d 8 49 9 14 9 38 10 02 10 26 10 50 11 14	5-25 am	As Mon.—Fri. until 12-15 pm	5-30 am 6 25 7 05 7 35 7 45 8 25 8 50 9 08 9 20d 9 32 9 56 10 20 10 44 11 08 11 32

(Grangetown route — North Ormesby to Grangetown)

then at Minutes past each Even hour: 2 18 26 34 42 50 58 / Odd hour: 6 22 30 38 46 54 — and every 10 mins. until — until — 8-50 pm and every 10 mins. until 10-40 pm / 10 50d 11 05d (d—to or from Depot)

Saturday: 5-30 am ... then at 4 mins past 19 34 49 each hour until 3 49 p.m. then 4-00 pm and every 10 mins. until 10-40 pm / 10 50d 11 05d

Sunday: 5-30 am ... until 10-40 pm / 10 50d 11 05d

(Grangetown to North Ormesby)

Monday—Friday 5-30 am ... and every 10 mins. until ... then at Minutes past each Even hour: 6 14 22 30 38 46 54 / Odd hour: 10 18 26 34 42 50 58 — until 8 54 p.m. then 9-00 pm and every 10 mins. until 10-30 pm / 10 40d 10 50d 11 00d

Sunday: 5-40 am ... then at 8 mins past 23 38 53 each hour until 4 06 p.m. then 4-20 pm and every 10 mins. until 10-30 pm / 10 40d 10 50d 11 00d

(North Ormesby to Normanby)

Monday—Friday 5-35 am ... and every 10 mins. until ... until 8 54 p.m. then 9-05 pm and every 10 mins. until 10-45 pm / 10 50d 11 05d

Saturday: then at 11 mins past 26 41 56 each hour until 3 56 p.m. then 4-05 pm and every 10 mins. until 10-45 pm / 10 50d 11 05d

(Normanby to North Ormesby)

Monday—Friday 5-25 am ... and every 10 mins. until ... and every 10 mins. until 9-05 pm and every 10 mins. until 10-45 pm / 10 35d 10 55d 11 05d

Saturday: until 8 58 p.m. then 9-05 pm and every 10 mins. until 10-45 pm / 10 35d 10 55d 11 05d

Sunday: then at 0 mins past 15 30 45 each hour until 4-15 pm and every 10 mins. until 10-45 pm / 10 55d 11 05d

PASSING TIMES from N. ORMESBY
CARGO FLEET OFFICES ... 5 mins. later
SOUTH BANK ... 9 "
CLEVELAND HOUSE ... 12 "
BAILEY'S CORNER ... 15 "

PASSING TIMES from GRANGETOWN
BAILEY'S CORNER ... 3 mins. later
CLEVELAND HOUSE ... 6 "
SOUTH BANK ... 8 "
CARGO FLEET OFFICES ... 12 "

PASSING TIMES from N. ORMESBY
CARGO FLEET OFFICES ... 5 mins. later
SOUTH BANK ... 9 "
LIBRARY ... 12 "
TEESVILLE ... 15 "

PASSING TIMES from NORMANBY
TEESVILLE ... 2 mins. later
LIBRARY ... 5 "
SOUTH BANK ... 8 "
CARGO FLEET OFFICES ... 12 "

THROUGH CARS — GRANGETOWN SQUARE TO NORMANBY

Monday to Thursday	Friday	Saturday	Sunday
7 20 am	7 20 am	12 03 pm	7 20 am
7 59	7 59		
8 28	8 30		
4 08 pm	12 02 pm		
5 04	12 15		
	12 30		
	12 35		
	12 45		
	1 05		
	1 15		
	1 25		
	1 35		
	1 55		
	2 05		
	2 25		
	4 08		
	5 03		
	5 25		
	5 45		

SPECIAL HIRE FACILITIES

Enquiries will receive IMMEDIATE ATTENTION

Write, call or phone 58666

YOUR OWN
SERVICE
AT YOUR
SERVICE

THROUGH CARS — NORMANBY TO GRANGETOWN SQUARE

Monday to Thursday	Friday	Saturday	Sunday
7 05 am	7 05 am	7 05 am	5 25 am
7 44	7 44		7 05 am
8 14	8 15		
8 45	8 40		
1 12 pm	12 10 pm		
4 49	12 17		
	12 30		
	12 45		
	1 00		
	1 10		
	1 20		
	1 30		
	1 40		
	1 50		
	2 10		
	2 20		
	4 48		
	5 30		
	5 40		

PRINTED BY JORDISON & CO., LTD., 8, MARTON ROAD, MIDDLESBROUGH.

GRANGETOWN

65.   East of Bennett's Corner, cars on the
Grangetown route ran alongside Dorman Long's
Cleveland Iron Works, whose blast furnaces
created a surreal backdrop to the trolleybuses.
TMT liveried car 1 approaches South Bank.
(Roy Brook)

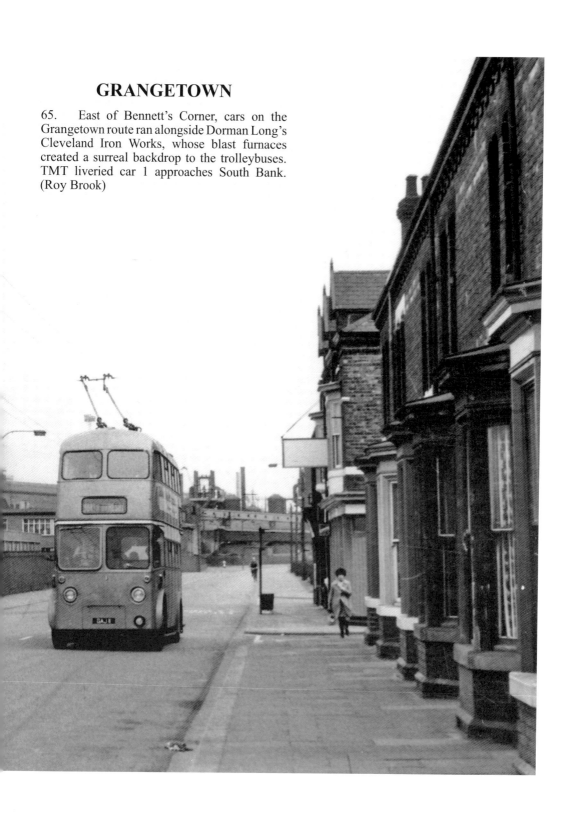

66.   Middlesbrough Road East continued into Eston Road at Cleveland House Corner. This was quite a long curve and was a prime spot for dewirements. The ex-Rotherham tower wagon is attending to damage to the overhead in January 1969, necessitating car 2 having to use the Grangetown–bound wires to continue its journey. The damage had been caused by a preserved Huddersfield trolleybus during a test run before operating an enthusiasts tour (see photograph 117). (P.Price)

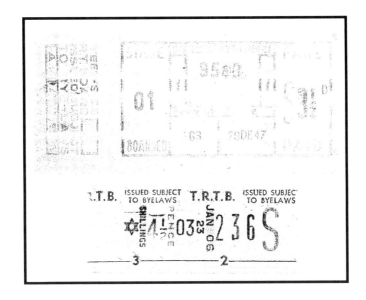

67.   In October 1965, car 15 has de-wired a
short distance west of the previous photograph.
Amazingly, the driver appears to have climbed
onto the car's roof, (doubtless by way of the
platform on the upper-deck emergency door), to
place the errant boom back on to the wire.
(M.J. Henderson)

68.   Eston Road ran parallel with the Dorman
Long's extensive private steelworks railway.
Utility car 11 heads for Grangetown on 25th
September 1959.   The railway is behind the
railings on the right. (J.Copland/A.D.Packer)

69. Proceeding in the opposite direction to photograph 68 is re-bodied car 18. The significance of this photograph is that it was taken on 1st January 1961, the first day that Roe re-bodied vehicles ran in service. In the middle distance the trolleybus route turns sharp left under the railway at the subway, whilst Eston Road runs on in the background into Church Lane leading to Eston village. In 1922, it had been proposed that the trolleybus route be extended along Church Lane to reach Eston. The bridge in the background carries the Trunk Road over Church Lane, and it also crossed the steelworks railway. (P.Battersby)

70. Car 6 descends below the railway and is about to make the turn into the subway. (J.Fozard)

71.   The subway consisted of a low bridge under the steelworks railway, combined with a steep ramp on the South Bank side of the bridge, and a right-angled bend into Eston Road. On 8th October 1953, utility car 18 emerges from the bridge, on which is standing one of Dorman Long's fleet of saddle-tank locomotives. (J.C.Gillham)

72.   Six years later, car 18, now re-built, is seen in the same location as the previous photograph. Note how little clearance there was between the vehicle roof and the bridge. It is operating a peak-hour working to Normanby. (J.Copland/A.D.Packer)

73.   Car 4 leaves the subway to proceed along Bolckow Road, Grangetown. Note the impressive railway signals and signal box-on this private line. (R.F.Mack)

The Bolckow Vaughan private railway

"In 1929, before acquisition by Dorman, Long and Co Ltd, the land occupied by the Cleveland Works of Bolckow, Vaughan and Co Ltd was 1,273 acres in extent, of which 252 acres were actually covered by buildings and plant. Within the works were 92 miles of standard gauge railway operated from signal cabins, 84 locomotives, 46 steam cranes, 3,100 wagons of various types, 350 furnace-charging cars and 140 slag ladles". Extract from 'Industrial Railway Record' (Journal of the Industrial Railway Society) – July 1963

74.   Here is a scene in Bolckow Road Grangetown, with car 2 pausing outside the Lyric Cinema. Grangetown had the local nickname 'Cardboard City', which derived from the post-war proliferation of temporary pre-fabricated housing in the area. (W.J.Haynes)

75.   The original Grangetown terminus was in the Market Square at the junction of Holden Street and Pochin Road, adjacent to the Literary Institute. The route from Bolckow Road was via Whitworth Road. Prototype Straker-Clough car 17 is seen negotiating the turning circle here in 1921. (Tramway and Railway World)

76.   By mid-1922, the Market Square terminus had been cut back to the junction of Whitworth Road and Holden Street. Here, car 15 waits at the turning circle on a journey to North Ormesby in September 1959. Local readers may remember the Amos Hinton grocery shop on the left. (J. Copland/A.D.Packer)

77.   By the late 1960s, workings to Grangetown Square were very much reduced, and they ceased altogether when the Eston extension opened. Car 5 is seen in the turning circle on a Normanby working. (P.Price)

⟶

78.   The wiring junction in Bolckow Road at Whitworth Road dated from April 1950 when the extension to Kingsley Road came into use. The overhead wires in Whitworth Road and the junction were removed altogether in early April 1968, just after the formation of TMT. Car 5 turns into Bolckow Road from Whitworth Road. (P.Price)

⟶

79.   This photograph, taken a year or so later than the previous one, shows that the wiring junction has gone. Ex-Reading car 11 passes Whitworth Road en route to North Ormesby. (C.Carter)

80. At Bailey's Corner, the route turned off Bolckow Road into Birchington Avenue, from where car 2 is seen negotiating the turn. This point was also commonly known as 'Lanny's Corner' after the popular café which is partly hidden behind the vehicle in this view. (J.Fozard)

81. Between Bailey's Corner and the terminus, Birchington Avenue crosses The Broadway. The roundabout at this junction can be seen in the background to this view of utility car 12 proceeding north. (Photobus)

82. Kingsley Road terminus was around an elongated island in Birchington Avenue known as the 'Bull Ring' and just short of the actual junction with Kingsley Road. The service terminated here from 1950 until 1964. Passengers have just alighted from car 1 at the setting-down stop at the 'Bull Ring'. Today, the housing in the background no longer exists and the land has been grassed over. (Photobus)

83.   A short extension to the Grangetown service, to serve the residents of the ever-expanding housing, came into use in June 1964. This took the route as far as the roundabout at the junction with Fabian Road. Passing along the new wiring towards Fabian Road is car 13, its destination blind already set for the return journey. Today, Grangetown Library occupies the left-hand side of the road at this point. (J.S.King)

84.   The Fabian Road terminus had a short life of under four years, becoming redundant when the Eston route was opened. Car 12 is about to negotiate the terminal loop at the roundabout at Fabian Road shortly after the extension was opened in June 1964. Tower wagon BAJ 846 is in attendance on the left. Trolleybuses were able to turn here for a short period after the extension to Eston until the turn-back wiring link was removed at the end of May 1968. (J.S.King)

ESTON - THE LAST TROLLEYBUS ROUTE

85.   Further housing development, and the long-held desire to link up the Grangetown and Normanby services via Eston, resulted in the construction of Britain's last trolleybus route in 1967–8. This remarkable view looking along Birchington Avenue towards Eston on 2nd January 1968 shows the trolleybus wiring in place before any housing had been built. (P.Battersby)

86.   Opening day. Car 3 made the first run over the new route on Sunday morning, 31st March 1968. Here, it waits at Fabian Road whilst steel shoes are fitted to the trolley-heads for wire cleaning purposes. Local children hold a ribbon across its path to 'launch' the new service. In the background, the visiting Brighton trolleybus is parked prior to carrying enthusiasts on a tour of the system. Car 3 ran to Eston Square, turned by gravity and returned to Fabian Road, cleaning the new wires en route. (C.Carter)

87. Between Fabian Road and Eston Road, Birchington Avenue climbs towards the Eston Hills in the background. At Whale Hill the carriageway splits around a grassed square. Here, car 13 proceeds north towards Grangetown during the construction of the housing. Car 13 was one of the first trolleybuses to be painted in the new TMT livery and ran for a time with a non-standard cream stripe below the lower–deck windows. (C.Carter)

88. Car 15 is seen at the top of Birchington Avenue, commencing the right turn towards Eston. (C.Carter)

89.   The right turn into Eston Road is protected by a short length of dual-carriageway, which allows vehicles to cross each carriageway separately. This view shows car T285 completing the right turn from Birchington Avenue into Eston Road on the last day of trolleybuses operation - Sunday, 18th April 1971, whilst operating a tour for the Omnibus Society. It had been given a full repaint prior to being handed over to Teesside Museums for preservation, including the unusual provision of the Teesside County Borough crest on its sides. (P.Battersby)

90.   Car 3 is seen in Eston Road approaching Eston Square. The short stretch of dual-carriageway road can be seen in the background. (J.S.King)

91.   The terminal stop at Eston Square for departures via Grangetown was outside the Miners Arms. Ex-Reading vehicle T289 is seen here. Note that the route number '91' is being displayed, indicating that this photograph was taken during the last week of trolleybus operation. The route numbers 90 (North Ormesby to Eston via Grangetown, returning via Normanby) and 91 (North Ormesby to Eston, via Normanby returning via Grangetown) were allocated to these services in readiness for motorbuses from 26th March 1971, but only the ex-Reading trolleybuses could display them. (Photobus)

TROLLEYBUS TIME TABLE

FROM 31st MARCH 1968 UNTIL FURTHER NOTICE.

NORTH ORMESBY — ESTON — NORTH ORMESBY

NORTH ORMESBY via GRANGETOWN to ESTON		ESTON via NORMANBY to NORTH ORMESBY		NORTH ORMESBY via NORMANBY to ESTON		ESTON via GRANGETOWN to NORTH ORMESBY	
Monday to Saturday	Sunday	Monday to Saturday	Sunday	Monday to Saturday	Sunday	Monday to Saturday	Sunday
0530	0530	0525	0531	0535	0542	0526	0539
and every 10 mins. until	then past even hour — odd hour 18 — 06 42 — 30 54 until 1706 then every 12 mins. until	and every 10 mins. until	then past even hour — odd hour 19 — 07 43 — 31 55 until 1731 then every 12 mins. until	and every 10 mins. until	then past even hour — odd hour 06 — 18 30 — 42 54 until 1712 then every 12 mins. until	and every 10 mins. until	then past even hour — odd hour 03 — 15 27 — 39 51 until 1715 then every 12 mins. until
2240	2242	2245	2243	2245	2248	2226	2233
2250d 2300d 2310d	2254d 2306d	2255d 2305d	2255d 2307d	2255d	2300d 2306d	2236d 2246d 2256d 2306d	2245d 2257d

d—to or from depot.

PASSING TIMES from N. ORMESBY		PASSING TIMES from ESTON		PASSING TIMES from N. ORMESBY		PASSING TIMES from ESTON	
SOUTH BANK	9 mins. later	NORMANBY	3 mins. later	SOUTH BANK	9 mins. later	GROSMONT ROAD	5 mins. later
BAILEYS CORNER	15 mins. later	TEESVILLE	5 mins. later	TEESVILLE	15 mins. later	BAILEY'S CORNER	10 mins. later
GROSMONT ROAD	20 mins. later	SOUTH BANK	11 mins. later	NORMANBY	18 mins. later	SOUTH BANK	16 mins. later

Circular Service
MONDAY TO FRIDAY

South Bank	Grangetown (Grosmont Road)	Eston	Normanby	South Bank
6.47	6.57	7.03	7.06	7.16
7.17	7.17	7.33	7.36	7.46
7.47	7.57	8.03	8.06	8.16
8.17	8.27	8.33	8.36	8.46
8.47	8.57	9.03	9.06	9.16
15.02	15.12	15.18	15.21	15.31
15.32	15.42	15.48	15.51	16.01
16.02	16.12	16.18	16.21	16.31
16.32	16.42	16.48	16.51	17.01

SPECIAL HIRE FACILITIES

Enquiries will receive

IMMEDIATE ATTENTION

Circular Service
MONDAY TO FRIDAY

South Bank	Normanby	Eston	Grangetown	South Bank
6.45	6.55	6.58	7.04	7.14
7.15	7.25	7.28	7.34	7.44
7.45	7.55	7.58	8.04	8.14
8.15	8.25	8.28	8.34	8.44
8.45	8.55	8.58	9.04	9.14
15.15	15.25	15.28	15.34	15.44
15.45	15.55	15.58	16.04	16.14
16.15	16.25	16.28	16.34	16.44
16.45	16.55	16.58	17.04	17.14

92.   Car 5 is at the Miners Arms terminus, Eston Square. It is possibly working on the short-lived 'Circular - N' peak-hour service from Bennett's Corner via Normanby to Eston, returning via Grangetown. Behind stands a United Bristol Lodekka en-route to Redcar. (S.Lockwood coll.)

93.   The terminus for departures via Normanby was in the one-way section of Eston Square itself, where car 12 is seen. The introduction of trolleybuses at this point resulted in the island here becoming a traffic roundabout, rather than a bus terminal operated in an anti-clockwise direction. This scene is on the first Saturday of operation of the Eston service. The vehicle also has the short-lived non-standard TMT livery with a cream stripe below the lower-deck windows. (J.S.King)

94.   Car 5 leaves Eston Square terminus on a journey to North Ormesby via Normanby. (C.Carter)

95.   Turning round from the previous photograph, car 13 approaches Eston Square from Normanby on 20th May 1968. (P.Battersby)

96.   The undulating High Street between Eston and Normanby is demonstrated by car 4 passing 'The Stapylton of Eston' public house. (C.Carter)

97.   Car 13 arrives at Normanby from Eston and is about to turn right into Normanby Road to rejoin the old route. The turning circle here was removed when the Eston extension opened. Note how the original overhead wiring fittings have been used to create the curve into the High Street, joining on to the new fittings of the extension. (S.Lockwood coll.)

Tees-side Railless Traction Board.

Councillor W. G. GRACE (Chairman).
THE MAYOR OF MIDDLESBROUGH (Councillor JOS. CALVERT),
Aldermen T. GIBSON POOLE and J. T. PANNELL,
Councillors T. M. SCOTT and JAS. POWELL.

OPENING CEREMONY

OF THE

Railless Traction Tramways,

Saturday, 8th November, 1919.

ORDER OF PROCEEDINGS.

1. When the Invited Guests have assembled at the Car Depot at 11 a.m., Councillor J. Fox, J.P., (Chairman of the Eston Urban District Council) will hand upon a Silver Salver the Controller Key, with which to drive the first official Car, to the Chairman of the Tees-side Railless Traction Board (Councillor W. G. Grace.)

2. The Chairman of the Board will then declare the Undertaking officially opened, and make some observations as to the inauguration of the Tramways.

3. The Right Worshipful The Mayor of Middlesbrough (Councillor Jos. Calvert, J.P.) will then move a Vote of Thanks to the Chairman of the Board for performing the Opening Ceremony, and this will be seconded by Major J. S. Crone, J.P., one of the Directors of the Trolley Vehicle Company, from whom the undertaking has been purchased.

4. The Chairman of the Board will then respond and proceed immediately thereafter to drive the first Car.

5. On returning to the Car Depot, the Guests are invited by the Board to partake of light Refreshments.

PRESTON KITCHEN,
Clerk to the Board.

Middlesbrough,
4th November, 1919.

ROLLING STOCK

98.   1 to 10 AJ 5857 to 5865

The inaugural 1919 fleet was ordered from the RET Construction Company, but following delays due to the difficulties described in the Historical Survey, the vehicles were supplied by Railless Ltd. Their chassis were actually built by the Cleveland Car Company of Darlington, with electrical equipment and the 28 seat rear entrance bodies supplied by English Electric. The parts were delivered to the South Bank depot and assembled there. Car 4 was withdrawn from service and dismantled by the Board in 1920, possibly to provide spares for the others. Apart from No. 4, registration numbers were allocated and carried from 1921. The remaining nine cars formed the mainstay of the fleet until being withdrawn in 1931 and 1932. This is car 6 in the grey-green livery of the original North Ormesby, South Bank, Normanby and Grangetown Railless Traction Company, in which these vehicles enter service. It is thought that the subsequent TRTB livery of the early cars (up to and including fleet number 22) was dark red and white.
(Teesside Archives)

99.   11 to 16 AJ 5866 to 5871

Six further cars joined the fleet in 1920, receiving North Riding registration marks in 1921. These were second-hand vehicles purchased from Clough, Smith and had originated with Rhondda Tramways Company. New in 1914, they had operated in Wales for only three months. Chassis and body were built by Brush, using Daimler chassis parts, and they had rear entrances and 26 seats. These vehicles carried the highly manoeuvrable Estler trolley gear with the poles mounted on top of each other, an arrangement which was adopted for all the Board's future trolleybus purchases until 1936. The open rear platforms of these vehicles were enclosed by a local South Bank coachbuilding firm soon after delivery to Tees-side. Cars 13 and 15 were withdrawn in 1926 and the others were out of service by 1928, although all were stored in operational condition until sold in 1929. This view is of car 11 outside the depot. Note the arrangement of the overhead wiring.
(Teesside Archives)

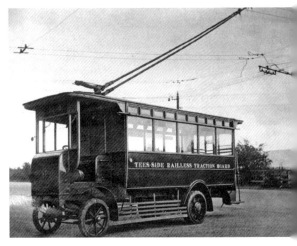

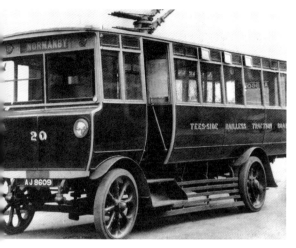

100. 17 to 21 AJ 7513, AJ 8607 to 8610

The TRTB General Manager, JB Parker, used the experience of operating the Railless and Brush cars to design the ideal trolleybus for the Tees-side operation. In partnership with Clough, Smith, a Straker-Squire motorbus chassis was adapted to his design. The result was the 'Straker–Clough' trolleybus chassis that developed into a very successful type during the 1920s, being sold to many fledgling trolleybus undertakings. The prototype was TRTB car 17, delivered in 1920 and carrying a Roe 36-seat body–a high capacity for that time. This was the first Roe trolleybus body. A further four (18 to 21) entered service the following year. These had a stepped frontal profile to their Roe bodies rather than the entirely flat front of car 17 (see photograph 4). (R.Marshall coll.)

101. 22 PY 1845

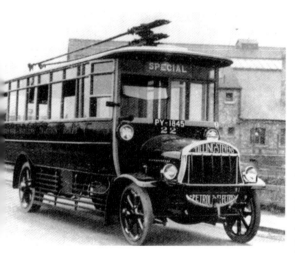

This vehicle was one of the most unusual trolleybuses to run in Britain and was another brainchild of the TRTB General Manager, this time to solve the problem of access to Eston, which was less than a mile from the Normanby terminus. It was built by Tilling-Stevens as a dual-mode vehicle using their Petrol-Electric chassis, but was fitted with trolley booms. Thus it was could run as a pure trolleybus directly feeding the motor from the overhead, in addition to its ability to run in petrol-electric mode away from the wires. The chassis designation was PERC1 (Petrol-Electric Railless Chassis type 1), and it carried a Roe front-entrance 32 seat body. Operation commenced in 1924 between North Ormesby and Eston, with a change of running mode at Normanby. Although the vehicle performed satisfactorily, it could not provide an acceptable frequency or reliability of service on its own, and the Board introduced motorbuses on a service to Eston via a different route in 1926. Thus car 22 spent most of its life in trolleybus mode, only venturing 'off-wire' on special occasions. It was withdrawn in 1936. Only one other chassis to this design was constructed, this being built in 1930 and supplied to Turin in Italy. (R.Marshall coll.)

102.   1 to 8 VN 3751 to 3758

The modernisation of the trolleybus fleet instigated by the Traffic Commissioner resulted in the entry into service in 1932 of eight Ransomes, Simms and Jeffries S4 chassis with 32 seat rear-entrance bodywork built by the same company. Their very modern appearance was in stark contrast to the Railless cars they replaced (see photograph 6). These vehicles were painted in a new livery of light blue with a broad white band at waist level, and it is believed that this livery also applied to the succeeding Leyland trolleybuses. During the Second World War, some of these vehicles ran painted in dull grey livery. The first withdrawal was in 1944 (car 6), and the others ran until 1949/50. This photograph of car 3 before delivery is of interest as it shows the vehicle on test on the Corporation trolleybus system at Ipswich, where Ransomes was based.
(AEI/J.S.King coll.)

103.   **9 to 13 VN 9434 to 9438**

      The delivery of these five vehicles in late 1936 permitted the withdrawal of the last remaining Straker cars plus the unique Tilling-Stevens hybrid. A new chassis make, Leyland, was introduced, these trolleybuses being of the TB3 type, which was the same as a demonstration vehicle operated during 1936 and referred to later in the book. Massey Brothers of Wigan supplied the 32 seat bodies, which included an internal bulkhead with a separate smoking area. The introduction of double-deck vehicles in 1944 allowed the Board to dispose of these vehicles prematurely. They were sold to Norths of Leeds (bus dealers), who quickly sold them on to Southend on Sea Corporation, where they ran until 1952. Car 10 is seen before delivery to Tees-side. (P.Battersby coll.)

104. **14 BVN 694**

The final single-deck trolleybus purchased by the Board in 1942 was this Sunbeam MF2A chassis with East Lancashire 32 seat rear entrance body, built to peacetime standards. The only single-decker built on an MF2A chassis, it had a short working life, being eclipsed by the introduction of the double-deck vehicles. It was surplus to requirements following the delivery of the 1950 Sunbeam F4s, and was stored in the depot yard until disposed of in 1957. This unique vehicle is seen in Normanby Road when new displaying wartime white marker paint around the lower body edge. It appears to be painted in the latter-day hedge–green livery that replaced the blue used by the trolleybuses delivered to the Board in the 1930s. (AEI/J.S.King coll.)

105. **10 to 13 PY 308 to 311** and **15 to 18 CPY 286 to 289**

The successful attempt by the Board to persuade the Ministry of Transport to allow double-deck operation resulted in the allocation of eight utility Sunbeam Ws, with Roe (10 to 13) or Weymann (15 to 18) bodies seating 56 passengers. They entered service between October 1944 and January 1945, the Weymann batch being first on the road. The first Weymann bodied vehicle to be delivered (car 15) proved to be slightly too high to negotiate the subway and this and the subsequent Weymann vehicles needed adjustments to bring the height to within the specified limit. The wooden seating of these vehicles was replaced by upholstered seats by 1949. All except car 11 were subsequently re-built by the Board in the late 1950s (see photograph 106) and then all were re-bodied by Roe between 1960 and 1962 (see photograph 108). This view shows car 17 at North Ormesby in the early 1950s. (H.Luff/Online Transport Archive/Photobus)

106.   **Utility Re-builds**

By 1957, the condition of the wartime utility bodies on the eight Sunbeam W trolleybuses was giving cause for concern, and a programme of re-building was instituted, starting with car 18. The process became rather protracted with some vehicles being off the road for quite a time, despite some of the work being contracted to Edmond, a local coachbuilder. The visible results of this process were the fitting of rubber-mounted windows with sliders rather than half-drop ventilation. This softened the harsh lines of the original product but a rather odd-looking vehicle was the result. All the utilities received this treatment between 1957 and 1960, apart from car 11, which, following accident damage, was sent instead for fitting with a brand-new body as detailed under photograph 108. Roe-bodied car 10 is seen at North Ormesby. (Photobus)

107. **1 to 7 GAJ 11 to 17**

The seven trolleybuses delivered in mid-1950 replaced the remainder of the single-deck fleet. They had Sunbeam F4 chassis with East Lancashire 56 seat bodies of composite construction. These were built at East Lancashire's Bridlington-based subsidiary. Visually, they resembled the East Lancashire metal framed trolleybus bodies supplied on BUT chassis to nearby Darlington a year earlier. The rear emergency window contained a platform for use by maintenance staff working on the trolley gear, and was therefore only partially glazed. In 1953, car 3 was decorated and illuminated for the Queen's Coronation, with a mainly silver livery (see photograph 114). All these vehicles were re-bodied by Roe between 1963 and 1965. This is car 5 at North Ormesby showing the original livery style carried by these vehicles. (D.A.Jones/London Trolleybus Preservation Society)

108. **1 to 7, 10 to 13, 15 to 18 Roe re-bodies**

Between 1960 and 1965, TRTB re-bodied the whole of its trolleybus fleet with CH Roe 61-seat rear-entrance bodies. These were to Roe's standard trolleybus design, which had already appeared on re-bodied chassis in other trolleybus fleets, i.e. Ashton-under-Lyne, Doncaster, Maidstone and Wolverhampton. The vehicles were sent to Roe's Leeds factory, generally in pairs, commencing with cars 11 and 18, which re-entered service on 1st January 1961, and the process ended when car 5 re-entered service in early 1965, bearing the last trolleybus body built for British service. Notable features on these Tees-side bodies were the cab door on the nearside only, and a circular illuminated panel below the rear platform window which when lit read 'Turning Circle' for use when negotiating the turning circles at termini. All except cars 10,11 and 15 were re-painted in TMT livery in 1968/9. Cars 10 and 12 were re-numbered 19 and 14 respectively in March 1969 following the delivery of the ex-Reading vehicles, although both were officially withdrawn shortly afterwards together with cars 11, 15 and 18. It is not thought that car 12 ever carried its new number. The remainder lasted until the end of the system, with cars 1 to 7 being re-numbered T281 to T287, and cars 13, 16 and 17 re-numbered T293/4/5 in August 1970. Car 2, shown here at Fabian Road, was preserved privately and is currently under restoration at the Trolleybus Museum at Sandtoft, in the hands of former TMT employee Peter Price. (S.Lockwood coll.)

109. **8 to 12 (T288 to T292) VRD 183 to 186, 192**

Five second-hand trolleybuses were purchased by Teesside Municipal Transport in early 1969 to modernise the fleet. They originated with Reading Corporation Transport, whose trolleybus system had closed in November 1968. The vehicles were new to Reading in 1961, being part of a batch of twelve numbered in the series 182 to 193 with the registration numbers matching the Reading fleet numbers. They had Sunbeam F4A chassis with Burlingham 68 seat forward entrance bodies and power doors. Their purchase was reportedly surrounded in controversy, TMT attempting at a late stage to withdraw from the sale and instead purchase ex-Bournemouth trolleybuses, which being slightly shorter in length would have been more manoeuvrable. Reading Transport insisted on the purchase being completed, and the vehicles were towed to Teesside in late January 1969. Interestingly this was carried out by a trolleybus enthusiast organisation, who by this time had gained considerable experience of towing preserved examples around the country. Fleet numbers 8 to 12 were allocated, and following painting in TMT livery, the vehicles entered service around the beginning of March. Their short life in the north–east was troublesome. Maintenance and reliability problems were common, and car 8 achieved only three months' service, being taken out of use in June 1969 following a major mechanical failure with car 12 suffering a similar fate a year later. Despite these withdrawals, the entire batch was re-numbered T288 to T292 in August 1970. Only cars T289 (formerly 9) and T291 (formerly 11) survived to the end of the system, the latter vehicle being painted in a commemorative livery for the closure ceremonies. This view shows car 11 at North Ormesby shortly after entering service and displaying an exterior advertisement. A limited amount of these appeared on the rear and sides of trolleybuses in the TMT era. (C.Carter)

Teesside Municipal Transport Undertaking

Memorandum

From: General Manager

To : Driver PW Price
South Depot

17th February 1969

All trolleybus drivers must acquaint themselves with the switches and controls of the new (ex-Reading Corporation) trolleybuses, as they are different from those presently in service. Driver/Instructor Mackey is available to give assistance to anyone wishing to familiarise himself with these vehicles, and it is intended to have one of them available to any driver wishing to handle it on the road.

Points to be noted
1) The new vehicles *are higher and extreme care is needed when travelling under the subway at Grangetown*
2) Booms are set approx. 2 ft. further back than on the older type of trolleybus, and allowance must be made for this fact, *particularly when negotiating North Ormesby turning circle and other sharp turns.*
3) Passenger doors must be closed before the vehicle can be moved from a bus stop.

Commencing 17th February 1969

The driving instructor will be available between :-
9.0 am   -   5.0 pm   Monday to Friday
9.0 am   -   12.0 noon   Saturday

Any member of staff requiring further information or driving tuition should avail himself.

After Friday 28th February 1969, if any member of the staff has not requested tuition, it will be assumed he is fully acquainted with the requirements.

WC Wilson
General Manager

TOWER WAGONS AT WORK

110.   During the latter years of the system, the Board's policy was to augment its tower wagon fleet by hiring-in suitable vehicles from former trolleybus operators, including West Hartlepool, Hull, Rotherham and, as depicted here, South Shields. CU 4039 was a 1938 Karrier made redundant by the closure of its home system in 1964. It is seen outside Cargo Fleet depot whilst involved in wiring alterations in connection with the 1966 diversion. Alongside is car 15 and above this can be seen the disconnected frog that once led to the outside siding (see photograph 31). (P.Battersby)

111   In late 1965, a red Bedford tower wagon, FET 196, was purchased by the Board from Rotherham Corporation. It is seen at work in South Bank in 1968 being passed by one of the Board's new Leyland Atlantean buses which were delivered in Teesside Municipal Transport livery in anticipation of the forthcoming merger. This is operating on the trolleybus service and is proceeding to North Ormesby, not Grangetown as shown. It is displaying the additional wording 'Trolley Service' on its blinds used for such trolleybus replacement workings and does not signify that at-seat refreshments are available !! (R.F.Mack)

FLEET NAMES AND FESTIVITIES

112.   This is a close–up of the distinctive fleet-name carried on the Board's vehicles between 1932 and 1968. Originally, this device was in golden yellow lettering with a clear background. From the late 1950s this was modified, the background colour becoming golden yellow with silver lettering. Note the hyphen in 'Tees-side'. (S.Lockwood coll.)

MUNICIPAL TRANSPORT

TEES-SIDE RAILLESS TRACTION BOARD

TROLLEYBUS TIME TABLE

FROM OCTOBER, 1965 UNTIL FURTHER NOTICE

GRANGETOWN ROUTE				NORMANBY ROUTE			
NORTH ORMESBY to GRANGETOWN		GRANGETOWN to NORTH ORMESBY		NORTH ORMESBY to NORMANBY		NORMANBY to NORTH ORMESBY	
Monday to Saturday	Sunday	Monday to Saturday	Sunday	Monday to Saturday	Sunday	Monday to Saturday	Sunday
0530	0530	0530	0540	0535	0515d 0520d	0525	0530
	0540 0550 0608 0625 0645 0705 0735 0745 0825 0904 0926 0950 1014 1038 1102 1120		0550 0605 0610d 0626 0703 0725 0755d 0805 0845 0920 0944 1008 1032 1056 1120		0605 0645 0655d 0725 0805 0838d 0849 0914 0938 1002 1026 1050 1114		0625 0705 0735 0745 0825 0850 0908 0920d 0932 0956 1020 1044 1108 1132
and		and		and		and	
every	then at 04 mins 19 past 34 each 49 hour until 1549 then	every	then at 08 mins 23 past 38 each 53 hour until 1606 then	every	then at 11 mins 26 past 41 each 56 hour until 1556 then	every	then at 0 mins 15 past 30 each 45 hour until
10		10		10		10	
mins.	1600 and every 10 mins. until	mins.	1620 and every 10 mins. until	mins.	1605 and every 10 mins. until	mins.	1615 and every 10 mins. until
until		until		until		until	
2240	2240	2230	2230	2245	2245	2245	2245
2250d 2305d	2250d 2305d	2240d 2250d 2300d	2240d 2250d 2300d	2250d 2305d	2250d 2305d	2235d 2255d 2305d	2255d 2305d
(d—to or from Depot)							

PASSING TIMES from N. ORMESBY
CARGO FLEET OFFICES ... 5 mins. later
SOUTH BANK ... 8 mins. later
CLEVELAND HOUSE ... 12 mins. later
BAILEY'S CORNER ... 15 mins. later

PASSING TIMES from GRANGETOWN
BAILEY'S CORNER ... 3 mins. later
CLEVELAND HOUSE ... 6 mins. later
SOUTH BANK ... 8 mins. later
CARGO FLEET OFFICES ... 12 mins. later

PASSING TIMES from N. ORMESBY
CARGO FLEET OFFICES ... 5 mins. later
SOUTH BANK ... 9 mins. later
LIBRARY ... 12 mins. later
TEESVILLE ... 15 mins. later

PASSING TIMES from NORMANBY
TEESVILLE ... 2 mins. later
LIBRARY ... 5 mins. later
SOUTH BANK ... 8 mins. later
CARGO FLEET OFFICES ... 12 mins. later

THROUGH CARS Grangetown to Normanby

Monday to Friday	Saturday	Sunday
0720	1203	0720
0759		
0828		
1202		
1608		
1704		

SPECIAL HIRE FACILITIES

Enquiries will receive

IMMEDIATE ATTENTION

Write, call or phone
Eston Grange 2166-7

YOUR OWN
SERVICE
AT YOUR
SERVICE

THROUGH CARS Normanby to Grangetown

Monday to Friday	Saturday	Sunday
0705	0705	0525
0744		0705
0814		
0840		
1312		
1649		

113.   This simplified variation of the fleet-name was carried on Ransomes car 5 seen at North Ormesby shortly after the Second World War. (W.J.Haynes)

114.   The Board entered into the festivities surrounding Queen Elizabeth's Coronation in 1953 by dressing up Sunbeam car 3 in a silver livery with red, white and blue trimmings, complete with 175 coloured lamps. It ran in service in this form for 10 days during the period. The depot frontage was also decorated as shown in the background to this photograph. (Teesside Archives)

STRANGERS IN THE CAMP

115.   In 1922, Railless Ltd tested this trolleybus on the Tees-side system. It was one of a batch of three, built by Railless with Roe 30-seat rear-entrance bodies for the Bloemfontein Municipal Tramways in South Africa. This view shows the vehicle at North Ormesby, proceeding towards the terminus, in January 1922.
(P.Battersby coll.)

116.   In the late 1960s, before transport museums with trolleybus running facilities had been established, organisations owning preserved trolleybuses were permitted by some surviving trolleybus operators to run private tours using these 'foreign' vehicles on their systems. To coincide with the opening of the Eston extension and the passing of TRTB, the Board allowed the operation of an enthusiasts' tour using ex-Brighton Hove and District No 6340, a 1939 AEC/Weymann trolleybus which was in the care of the London Trolleybus Preservation Society, and had not run under its own power since 1959. It operated a tour of the system on 31st March 1968, the last day of the Board's existence. On the previous day, it ran on test from the depot to Grangetown Square and back and it is seen turning out of Whitworth Road into Bolckow Road on what would have been one of the last visits by a trolleybus on this section. The Whitworth Road wiring was removed a few days later. (S.Lockwood/Photobus)

117.   A second tour involving a preserved trolleybus took place on Sunday 12th January 1969, when the West Riding Trolleybus Society operated ex-Huddersfield 619 on the system. This vehicle was a six-wheel 30 foot long BUT/East Lancashire 72 seater. The turning circle at North Ormesby could only be used by resorting to a shunt mid-way round, but the rest of the system, including the subway at Grangetown and the reverser at South Bank (as seen here), was successfully negotiated. Note the upward bend to the tip of the negative (nearside) trolley boom. This adjustment was necessary to allow the vehicle to pass through the subway without de-wiring. The author can be seen on the extreme right apparently contemplating the overhead wiring. (P.Price)

More strangers

Demonstration vehicles

From time to time, demonstation trolleybuses ran on the TRTB system for varying lengths of periods. These were:

UK 9601 – Guy BT Single-deck rear-entrance with 32 seats. This vehicle ran during December 1930.

TJ 2822 – Leyland TB3 Single-deck centre-entrance with 32 seats. This vehicle operated for one year between December 1935 and December 1936, allowing overhauls to take place of the existing fleet. Presumably this demonstration led to the chassis order for cars 9 to 13.

NBB 628 – British United Traction/Metro-Cammell–Weymann Q1 double-deck, three axle. Newcastle Corporation No. 628. Although not officially recorded, there is anecdotal evidence that this vehicle paid a brief visit to Tees-side in late 1950 on its delivery run to Newcastle after being exhibited at the Commercial Motor Show in London. It is reported that it was unable to pass under the subway bridge and could not negotiate the North Ormesby turning circle safely. It did not run in passenger service. The vehicle still exists at the East Anglia Transport Museum.

Second-hand chassis

FWX 909, 910 – Formerly Mexborough and Swinton Sunbeam F4 trolleybuses (Originally M&S fleet Nos. 25 and 26 with single-deck Brush bodies).

These chassis, bought in 1961 were to be fitted with new Roe double-deck bodies for service at Tees-side. This was never done and the chassis were gradually dismantled at South Bank depot for spare parts.

118.   Less than a week after the visit of the Huddersfield trolleybus, another stranger arrived, but in this case its visit became more permanent, and four others soon followed it. On Saturday, 18th January 1969, ex-Reading trolleybus 185, the first of the quintet purchased by TMT arrived at Tees-side. The opportunity was taken on the following day to run an enthusiasts' tour with the vehicle still in Reading livery. It is seen here at North Ormesby during a test run prior to the tour. (J.Banks coll.)

FINALE

119.   The last day of public service was on Sunday, 4th April 1971. For much of the morning, a full normal service of four trolleybuses was achieved, using cars T282, T285, T289 and T291, plus T281 used briefly as a duplicate to cope with demand. T291 had been painted in a special livery, with the upper-deck panels all around the body being devoted to valedictory messages and symbols. It had entered service in this form on the previous Thursday. All the trolleybuses were taken out of service and replaced by motorbuses from midday onwards, although in the afternoon, enthusiasts' tours took place. This is the scene at North Ormesby, when the cars congregated before operating their last journeys in public service. Car T285 is on the left with car T281 in front of it and decorated car T291 at the loading stop on the right. (P Price)

120. The formal closure of the Tees-side trolleybus system did not take place until a fortnight after the public service had ceased. On Sunday 18th April, trolleybuses once again appeared on the streets, commencing with enthusiasts' tours run by the National Trolleybus Association (using T289) and The Omnibus Society (using freshly re-painted T285). In the afternoon, the official last trolleybus procession took place and consisted of T285 and T282 carrying enthusiasts and T291 at the rear carrying the invited civic party. The route taken was from the depot to Eston via Normanby, returning via Grangetown. A prolonged stop was made in Normanby Road at Eston Sports Centre where T285 was formally handed over to Teesside Museums. By 4.30pm the cars had arrived back at the depot. This view shows the last official movement of the Tees-side trolleybus, as crowds watch decorated car T291 reversing into the depot for the last time. Fifty-one years earlier, their forebears had watched Railless car 10, the ceremonial first car, emerging from that very same doorway seen in photograph no. 1. (J.S.King)

MP Middleton Press

Easebourne Lane, Midhurst, West Sussex.
GU29 9AZ   Tel:01730 813169

EVOLVING THE ULTIMATE RAIL ENCYCLOPEDIA

www.middletonpress.co.uk   email:info@middletonpress.co.uk
A-0 906520   B-1 873793   C-1 901706   D-1 904474

OOP Out of Print at time of printing - Please check current availability   **BROCHURE AVAILABLE SHOWING NEW TITLES**